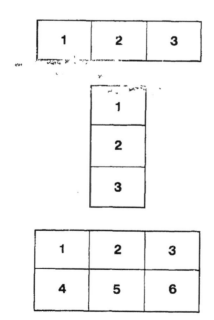

CASE OF

Progressive Pernicious Anæmia

(IDIOPATHIC OF ADDISON.)

BY

WILLIAM GARDNER, M.D.,

PROFESSOR OF MEDICAL JURISPRUDENCE,
McGILL UNIVERSITY;

AND

WILLIAM OSLER, M.D., L.R.C.P. LOND.,

PROFESSOR OF INSTITUTES OF MEDICINE,
McGILL UNIVERSITY.

———

Reprinted from CANADA MEDICAL AND SURGICAL JOURNAL, *March,* 1877.

———

Montreal:
PRINTED AT THE "GAZETTE" PRINTING HOUSE.

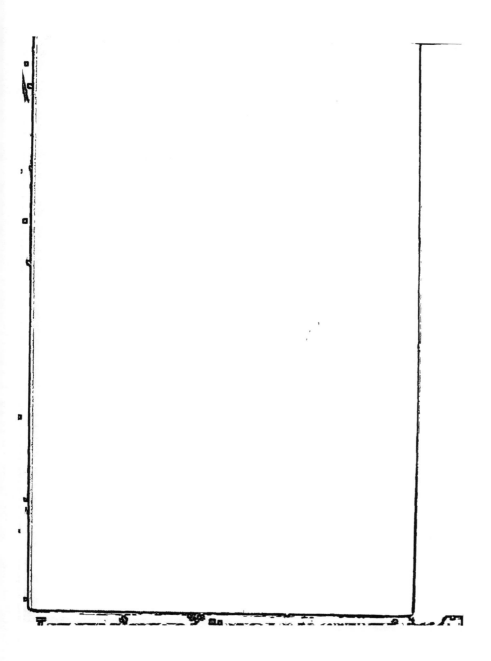

CASE OF

Progressive Pernicious Anæmia

(IDIOPATHIC OF ADDISON.)

BY

WILLIAM GARDNER, M.D.,

PROFESSOR OF MEDICAL JURISPRUDENCE.
McGILL UNIVERSITY;

AND

WILLIAM OSLER, M.D., L.R.C.P. LOND.,

PROFESSOR OF INSTITUTES OF MEDICINE,
McGILL UNIVERSITY.

Reprinted from CANADA MEDICAL AND SURGICAL JOURNAL, *March,* 1877.

Montreal:
PRINTED AT THE "GAZETTE" PRINTING HOUSE.

A CASE OF

PROGRESSIVE PERNICIOUS ANÆMIA.

(IDIOPATHIC OF ADDISON.)

The following case occurring in the practice of Dr. Gardner, is recorded as a contribution to the literature of a disease, rare, but by no means new, in any sense, concerning the pathology of which we have still a good deal to learn, and concerning the succesful treatment of which we as yet know nothing.

G. A., æt. 52, a native of England, employed in a spike factory, first came under observation on the 5th November, 1876. He is a thin, spare, moderately well-built man of average stature, and with gray hair and beard.

He is one of a large family, all of whom, except some who died in infancy, are now alive. His mother was very subject to diarrhœa. All of the family have had at one time or another serious illnesses, which, however, in their nature, have no bearing on the present case. Two or three members of the family have had a tendency to bleeding at the nose.

At the age of between six and seven, shortly after coming to
Canada, he had a long illness of five or six months duration,
the nature of which, beyond the fact that it was attended with
fever of remittent type, could not be ascertained. After
recovering from this illness, he continued to be very healthy
and active, suffering from little except somewhat frequent, slight,
and easily-controlled bleedings from the nose. He never had
had free bleeding from slight wounds. He was, however, subject
to occasional attacks of diarrhœa. During the last few years
he had occasional attacks of lumbago, and pains in some of his
joints. None of these complaints prevented him for more than
a few days from continuing his employment, which, until within
some months previous to his being laid up, involved a great deal
of muscular exertion.

About five years ago he lost, within three months, the only
two sons of his family, and his friends assert that, although he
did not display much emotion, he took the bereavement very
much to heart, and that since then his health has greatly failed,
that in particular he has become weaker and lost colour.

Nearly two years ago this became so decided, that his friends
induced him to go away for change of air. He accordingly
went to Toronto on a visit to a sister. During the first few days
he felt better, but after exposure to cold and wet he was seized
with an illness, setting in with rigors, and attended with cough,
bloody sputa, and delirium. This illness lasted a fortnight,
and was called by his medical attendant congestion of the lungs.

Ever since this illness he has been gradually growing paler
and weaker, and liable during the summers, especially that of
1876, to frequent diarrhœa, never very severe, but rather
constant. He would often have in the morning one or two loose
motions, and during the day have no further trouble from it.

The symptoms of which he specially complained were
weakness, attacks of shortness of breath, when he walked
in the cold air, especially if he faced a wind, and diarrhœa—
five or six motions in each twenty-four hours. Notwithstand-
ing these symptoms he had been attending regularly to his
occupation, which, however, did not involve much muscular

exertion. At this time the most striking feature of his case was a remarkable waxy pallor of the skin and mucous membranes, and a pearly appearance of the white of the eyes. He is somewhat deaf; this he attributes to his occupation in a noisy workshop.

Pulse rather more frequent than normal; temperature normal. Appetite by his own account and that of his friends, is good—he is able to eat meat; suffers no distress after food. Sleeps very soundly, and sleeps a great deal, much more than previous to the failure of his health. If he sits down and is let alone he is sure to go asleep. Is compelled to be up two or three times each night to make water. Urine very highly coloured; quantity in twenty-four hours thirty-four to forty ounces; specific gravity varied from 1012 to 1016 at different times; no albumen; no sugar; no bile pigment; no tube casts.

Complains of some numbness of his fingers, hands and forearms; has difficulty in buttoning his clothes, or in using his tools. Complains of a throbbing, rushing sensation in his temples. Says that he has suffered from decided diarrhœa for rather more than a month, but the number of motions in each twenty-four hours has not exceeded five or six. They have been painless and free from blood. Physical examination of the chest reveals nothing abnormal. The superficial cardiac dulness is normal in extent; the apex-beat natural in position; heart-sounds not specially changed—the first sound perhaps less accentuated than normal. There is a distinct bruit in the vessels of the neck and upper part of the chest.

The spleen is normal in size, or at all events not enlarged; the liver not enlarged.

The most careful examination reveals nowhere any pigmentation or bronzing of the skin. There is not the slightest evidence of enlargement of any of the superficial lymphatic glands. The symptom of which he complained most was the shortness of breath, which, as already mentioned, came on when he attempted to walk facing a wind, and was so urgent as to compel him to stop for a minute or two till he recovered his breath.

The liq. ferri pernitratis was prescribed in doses of fifteen minims in a wine glassful of water three times a day, and also a diet from which vegetables and fruits were to be excluded. At the end of a week he returned to say that his diarrhœa had almost ceased, and that he fancied himself a little better. As on the previous occasion, he had walked from his house—fully three-quarters of a mile. There was no other change to note in the symptoms.

He continued to come regularly at intervals of a week for the next three weeks. During this time the diarrhœa had entirely left him ; he was, he said, eating fairly, yet he was growing steadily weaker. The numbness of the fingers, hands and forearms was more marked, the difficulty in buttoning his clothes greater, the throbbing and rushing sensations in the head more distressing and the drowsiness more troublesome. A loud systolic bruit, much intensified by exertion, had developed in the region of the heart, loudest at the base, but heard also at the apex. The murmur in the vessels of the neck had become exceedingly loud.

At this time there was no œdema of face or ankles. The attacks of dyspnœa had been much mitigated by wearing a respirator over the mouth on going into the cold air.

He continued to take the pernitrate of iron during the first three weeks, but the only effect noticed from its use, if, indeed, it deserves the credit, was the cessation of the diarrhœa. The ammonio-citrate was then given instead for the next two weeks, but without the least benefit. Cod liver oil was next prescribed, but it disagreed so markedly that it was discontinued at once. He had not been seen for a fortnight, when, on the 29th December, a message was received asking that he should be seen at his house. There was little change to note in his condition, other than an intensification of the symptoms previously noted. The pallor was more intense, the weakness greater, the drowsiness and deafness more marked, but in addition there was slight œdema of the ankles and eyelids. Vallet's pills were now prescribed and taken for a week, but without the slightest benefit, as he continued to grow steadily weaker and worse, being scarcely able to leave his bed. On the evening of the 11th January of the present year, an urgent message to see him was received. On reaching his house it was found that on being assisted out of bed to make water, he had had an attack, apparently syncopal in its nature, and that at times, especially when left to himself, he was rambling and incoherent. He, however, answered questions correctly. He was very restless; pulse 110, temperature 102°. He had also been vomiting.

Jan. 12*th.*—Noon—Temperature has fallen to 101°. Other symptoms as at last report. Dr. Howard, Professor of Medicine, McGill University, saw him in consultation at this visit, and fully concurred in the diagnosis.

At 10 p. m. the pulse was 105 and the temperature 97·5° Retention of urine, requiring the use of the catheter. Urine very high-colored, red-brown, acidity normal, no albumen, sugar or bile-pigment ; specific gravity, 1016.

Jan. 13*th.*—11 a. m.—Pulse 98, temperature, 97·3°. Not so restless, still incoherent ; vomits everything ; catheter has to be introduced regularly.

Jan. 14*th.*—Died at 3 a. m.

The blood examined during life presented the following appearances in a specimen obtained, in a capillary tube, fifteen hours before death, and examined without the addition of any reagent, 30″ after withdrawal. (Hartnack, No. 9 im. and Oc. 3.)

About one-half of the red blood corpuscles run together to form rouleaux. The majority of them appear of large size, but do not present the characteristic round contours of these bodies ; many are ovoid, others lozenge-shaped, or of various forms, with irregular projections and processes. Isolated corpuscles look of the natural pale yellow colour, but the alternating light and dark centre with the change of focus is not so distinct as usual. On touching the top cover and causing them to roll over, many do not present the biconcave appearance, but look thin and flattened out. A limited number are crenated. In each field certain small round red corpuscles are seen, sometimes as many as six or eight. They are spheres, not biconcave, of a pale yellow colour, occasionally crenated or irregular in form.

The measurements of some of the coloured elements are given below (Hartnack No. 16 im.), from which an accurate idea is obtained of the remarkable discrepancies in size. About forty measurements were made of corpuscles taken at random in two or three specimens obtained a few days before death. Of these one was $\frac{1}{1233}''$ by $\frac{1}{2070}''$, being somewhat elongated. Five ranged from $\frac{1}{2150}''$ to $\frac{1}{2113}''$, these being the extremes. In twenty-two the range was from $\frac{1}{3000}''$ $\frac{1}{4700}''$ to In this group the usual looking red disks occurred. In five the diameter varied from between $\frac{1}{5000}''$ and $\frac{1}{6000}''$. In five the diameter was less than the $\frac{1}{5000}''$, the lowest being $\frac{1}{8374}''$.

Prolonged examination failed to discover a single nucleated red corpuscle.

The colourless corpuscles did not appear relatively increased. One or two were seen in each field of the No. 9 and 3. The measurements in five corpuscles ranged from $\frac{1}{2100}''$ to $\frac{1}{1700}''$. They were quite natural looking, and displayed a remarkable degree of vitality. In a slide mounted and surrounded with paraffine at 1 P.M., the amœboid movements were very active, the temperature of the room being about 60°.[*] At 7 P.M. the slide was carried in the hand a distance of a quarter of a mile to the house of a friend (temperature 14.2° F.), and the irregular changes in outline were still observed, and continued until 8:40, when the observation was omitted. There was an entire absence of Schultze's granular masses.

Autopsy.—Thirty-two hours after death.

Body that of a well-built man of fair muscular development. Hair grey. No emaciation; panniculus adiposus well developed, especially over abdomen. Skin of extraordinary pallor,

---

[*] It may be here mentioned that the statement of Ranvier, Traite d'Histologie (p. 210), that the amœboid movements of white blood corpuscles do not go on at ordinary temperatures is incorrect. In University sity College Laboratory, London, it was found on one occasion that the amœboid movement contined in the colourless corpuscles twenty-four hours after removal from the body. The blood was sealed in a capillary tube, and remained at the ordinary temperature in the month of June.

W. O.

with slight lemon tint, the shoulders marked with patches of deeper yellow hue. A few old psoriasis spots seen in the region of the elbows and knees. No petechiæ. Lineæ albicantiæ in the skin of groins, and upper and outer aspect of thighs, and on the outer edge of anterior folds of axillæ. Fingers slightly clubbed, and the nails of both hands markedly incurvated. Rigor mortis moderately well marked. Post mortem stains scarcely perceptible. No enlargement of the superficial lymphatic glands. No cadaveric odour.

Brain.—Not examined.

On making the preliminary incision a layer of deep yellow fat, fully an inch in thickness, is cut through over the abdomen. Muscles of the thorax of a remarkably healthy red colour. In the abdominal cavity the position of the viscera normal. Omentum moderately fatty. In the thorax a considerable amount of fat over the pericardium. The left pleural sac contains twelve ounces of bloody, yellowish-tinged, serum. A few strong adhesions posteriorly. In the right pleural sac ten to twelve ounces of fluid of the same character. Adhesions more numerous at apex and sides.

Pericardium.—Contains six drachms of a yellowish, bloody serum. No ecchymoses on either leaf.

Heart.—Large, excessively flabby. Sub-pericardial fat abundant about the base and in the anterior ventricular groove. Patch of attrition over upper part of right ventricle in front, and another behind, near the inferior vena cava. On opening the heart in situ an ounce of blood, with one small coagulum, in the cavities of the right side, and ten drachms in those of the left. Organ flaccid, and walls collapsed when laid on the table. Right auricle normal. Right ventricle somewhat dilated, the endocardium stained by imbibition. Tricuspid valves a little thickened and gelatinous at the edges; orifice of normal size. Pulmonary semi-lunar valves healthy, one segment fenestrated. Cavity of left ventricle large, walls of normal thickness. Mitral valves quite healthy, a little stained; orifice of proper size. Aortic semi-lunar valves a little opaque; slight atheroma at their bases, and on the aorta opposite their

free borders   Sinuses of Valsalva very distinct.   Nothing
abnormal in the left auricle.   Muscle substance of the organ
exceedingly pale, having a yellowish, faded-leaf appearance,
especially marked in the walls of the left ventricle.

Aorta.; both arch and trunk of full size.   Beyond the left
sub clavian there is a flattened patch of atheroma, about the size
of a half-penny.

Lungs—Deeply pigmented, crepitant throughout, lower
lobes œdematous and dark in colour posteriorly   The mucous
membrane of the *Trachea* at the bifurcation, and extending
irregularly nearly to the larynx, is represented by a number of
bony plates, lying immediately upon the cartilages, which are
themselves very dense, and partially ossified.

Spleen—Weight, six ounces, soft and flabby   Capsule a
little opaque   On section, pulp soft, of a light brownish-red
colour.   Trabeculæ distinct.   Malpighian corpuscles not evident   Very little blood in the organ ; none could be obtained
from the splenic vein.

Left Kidney.—Length, 5 ″   Unusual amount of superficial
fat.   Capsule loosely attached, and on removal leaves a very
anæmic-looking organ.   No atrophy of the cortex, which is
pale and bloodless   Pyramids, except at the bases, also pale
Right Kidney, 4½ ″ long, dark red in colour, uniformly con-
gested, forming a striking contrast to the other.   Capsule easily
detached ; stellate veins prominent.   On section, both cortex
and medulla contain much blood.

Supra-renal Capsules—The right is soft in the centre, and
somewhat larger than the left, but nothing unusual about
either.

Bladder—Distended with pale urine   Mucous membrane
healthy looking.   Prostate gland of full size.

Tonsils and glands at root of tongue not enlarged.   Several
ecchymoses beneath the mucous membrane of the anterior wall
of the pharynx.   *Œsophagus* presents nothing unusual ; a few
small extravasations are noticed near the cardia.

Mucous membrane of *stomach* pale, and at the cardiac end
thin ; at the pylorus it is thicker   *Duodenum* healthy , common

bile duct is pervious. *Jejunum* contains a quantity of dirty yellow mucus. Mucous membrane is pale. In the *ileum*, Peyer's patches are scarcely perceptible; the solitary glands towards the ileo-cæcal valve are alone distinct. In the *large bowel* the mucous membrane is anæmic. No ulceration. Scybalæ in transverse and descending colon.

Liver.—Rather small, of a light yellow colour, especially in the left lobe. Capsule smooth. On section a small quantity of liquid blood is seen in some of the hepatic veins. In places there is a very slight injection of the intra-lobular veins, which relieves the otherwise uniformly pale surface.

Gall-bladder.—Full of dark tarry bile.

Pancreas.—Looks healthy.

Abdominal blood-vessels almost entirely empty. No blood in inferior vena cava or aorta. Intima of both healthy-looking. *Thoracic Duct* pervious throughout. Mesenteric and retro-peritoneal *lymphatic glands* small, the former unusually so, requiring considerable searching to obtain any. The amount of blood in the body appeared remarkably diminished, and it was only by pressing along the limbs that sufficient could be obtained from the veins to fill a small homœopathic phial.

Piece of the sternum, the upper half of right fibula, the inner third of left clavicle, half a rib, and one of the last dorsal vertebræ were removed for the examination of the marrow. Blood was collected from the heart, and junction of left jugular vein with the sub-clavian.

A striking feature in the autopsy is the extreme anæmia of the organs, their almost entire bloodlessness, and consequent pallor, the right kidney excepted

HISTOLOGICAL EXAMINATION.

The blood taken from heart and veins shows the same general characters noticed during life. Prolonged examination of different specimens made for this special object resulted in the detection of two nucleated red blood corpuscles.

Heart.—The fibres are in a condition of extreme fatty degeneration, the striæ being obscured by the number of densely crowded droplets and fine molecular fat, only here and there a fibre occurs in which the striæ are faintly seen In teased preparations numerous short bits occur, together with oil-drops and granules of fatty matter In places there appears to be a good deal of interfibrillar connective tissue with fat cells

Muscles of the Trunk.—The fibres of the thoracic muscles—which were observed to be of such a natural appearance—present no trace of fatty degeneration

Spleen.—The ordinary corpuscles of the pulp, together with elongated, sometimes branched, cells of the retiform tissue are the chief elements seen in teased specimens The red corpuscles have lost their colouring matter A few cells containing red blood corpuscles are seen, but no nucleated red cells.

Kidney—Teased preparations show the epithelium of the tubules, both in the cortex and pyramids, covered with fatty matter in the form of minute drops and fine granules ; nowhere, not even in the large collecting tubes, are the cells distinct The Malpighian corpuscles also contain many granules and small oil-drops, and the same exist abundantly in the field.

Liver—Cells are stuffed with oil-drops, none noticed without them, while in many the protoplasm and nucleus are entirely obscured. Free fat exists infiltrated between the cells, and in the field In a few, bile pigment is seen

Mesenteric Glands—Teased portions present a large number of perfectly normal-looking lymph corpuscles, among which the connective tissue elements occur in the usual proportion. Many of the small vessels and capillaries have their walls uniformly studded with fat grains, and may be traced as dark branching lines. In others, the deposition is not so extensive

Nothing abnormal observed in the axillary lymphatic glands.

Medulla of Bones—The marrow of all the bones examined—sternum, rib, clavicle, vertebra, fibula—is of a dark violet-red colour, thick, about the consistence and colour of the spleen pulp in fever. In the clavicle it is more diffluent, of a lighter red colour, and to the naked eye looks a little fatty—an appearance not noticeable in the other bones, not even in the shaft of the fibula

On microscopical examination, the following elements were found :—

(1) Colourless corpuscles—marrow cells—of various size, with granular protoplasm, and bold vesicular nuclei. The greater number of these are larger than white blood corpuscles, and usually have a single nucleus, sometimes two. Others are smaller, more approaching the blood corpuscles in form, while in all the specimens examined, small round cells, like ordinary lymph corpuscles, are also found. The above represent the common colourless elements found in marrow, and they form the majority of the corpuscles in the field. In eight of the larger cells the extremes of measurements were $\frac{1}{1571}''$ by $\frac{1}{1311}''$ and $\frac{1}{1700}''$ by $\frac{1}{3335}''$.

(2) Coloured blood corpuscles, of which two varieties are seen ; (a) ordinary biconcave disks, somewhat irregular in shape, and often, as noticed in the blood during life, provided with long processes. They are abundant, forming the large proportion of coloured elements. In the fibula, sternum, and rib the colouring matter is retained, while in the vertebra and clavicle it has disappeared from most of the corpuscles, and they are recognizable only as outlines. (b) Small round red corpuscles, non-nucleated, from one-quarter to one-half the size of ordinary corpuscles, and similar in appearance to the small forms seen in the blood. They occur most numerously in the marrow of the fibula, where they form fully one-fourth of the coloured corpuscles. In the sternum and ribs they are not so abundant, though occurring in each field. As described in the blood itself, they do not appear to be biconcave disks, but spheres. The colouration is quite as intense as in form a, and a few were observed to be crenated.

(3) Nucleated red corpuscles, the " transitional " forms of Neumann, which are numerous in the sternum and rib, less so in the fibula, while in the clavicle and vertebra they occur scantily, or, owing to the general decolourization of the red corpuscles in these bones, are seen with difficulty. As shown by the measurements given below, they are as a rule larger than ordinary blood corpuscles, but present, like them, a perfectly homogene-

ous coloured stroma, in which a finely granular nucleus is imbedded. They are spheres, not biconcave, as a rule round, though frequently irregular in outline, or with one end pointed and prolonged. The intensity of the colouration in most cases equalled that of the ordinary red corpuscles, in some instances being deeper, in others not so marked. The nuclei are either round or elliptical, and occupy from one-quarter to one-half of the body of the cell (see measurements). They are solid, granular, and inside the corpuscle look coloured, though not so deep as the surrounding substance. The presence of nucleolus could not be determined. The position in the cells is variable ; in specimens examined within a short time after the post-mortem they appeared to be chiefly centric, but in preparations taken the next day very many of them had become quite peripheral, while others had protruded almost through the corpuscle, when it could be clearly seen that the nucleus was colourless. In several instances the nuclei are seen to be entirely outside the cells, though remaining attached to them. In this condition they look not unlike the small lymphoid marrow cells, and it is only the large size of the corpuscles to which they adhere, and the fact that in the same field others may be seen half-way out, that enables a correct opinion to be formed. In three or four instances dumb-bell-shaped nuclei were noticed. Cells with two nuclei were not uncommon, and instances with three and four were observed. As remarked above, the nucleated red forms are numerous in the sternum and rib, six to eight being seen at once in the field of the No. 9 im. and 3, while in the fibula not more than three or four were noticed in any single field. In fifteen measurements of these forms, eleven were above the $\frac{1}{2000}''$; five being $\frac{1}{1848}''$. The following measurements are of three corpuscles with their contained nuclei :— (1) $\frac{1}{1414}''$ by $\frac{1}{1400}''$; nucleus $\frac{1}{2818}''$ by $\frac{1}{2486}''$. (2) $\frac{1}{2300}''$ by $\frac{1}{2331}''$; nucleus $\frac{1}{3308}''$ by $\frac{1}{2000}''$. (3) $\frac{1}{2037}''$ by $\frac{1}{1764}''$; nucleus $\frac{1}{3556}''$ by $\frac{1}{3434}''$. A good idea of the irregularity in outline of these corpuscles and the slightly elliptical character of the nuclei may be gathered from the above.

(4) Cells containing red blood corpuscles. These are very

abundant in the marrow of the vertebra, three or four occurring in the field at once, and containing from five to six red corpuscles, the colour and outlines of which in most cases are preserved.　In the sternum and rib they are not nearly so numerous ; in the fibula and clavicle they were not observed.

(5) Myeloplaques, of which one or two only were met with in the marrow of the sternum and rib.　Neither in the shaft nor epiphysis of the fibula could these forms be determined.

(6) Fat cells, which are present in marrow of the clavicle in small numbers, absent in the sternum, vertebra and rib.　In marrow from the fibula an oil-drop is occasionally met with in the field, but here also they are almost entirely absent.

(7) The octahedra crystals, first described by Charcot, and which always occur in the marrow from twelve to thirty-six hours after death.

REMARKS.—Apart from the clinical features and general pathological appearances of the above case, which show it to be an exceedingly typical one, there are two points of special interest, viz., the appearance of the blood, and the condition of the bone marrow, both of which are deserving of a few comments.

Prof. Eichorst has drawn attention in a short note* to the presence in the blood of patients suffering with pernicious anæmia of exceedingly small red corpuscles, which he regards as pathognomonic of the disease, and affording a valuable diagnostic sign, being present in all of his cases, seven in number. The following are his own words :

" Some of the red globules are of normal size, but very pale and have lost their tendency to form rouleaux, others scarcely attain $\frac{1}{4}$ the diameter of a normal, perfect corpuscle, so that they look like small drops of fat tinged red, and have not their biconcave appearance."　Towards the latter stages of the disease he states that they increase, so that before death they may equal in number the common forms.

The histological examination, both before and after death,

* Centralblatt f. die. Med. Wissen. June 24th, 1876.

and the measurements above given, show that in this instance
the blood did contain an unusual number of small coloured
elements, and is so far confirmatory of Eichorst's statement.
Though not abundant, they were quite numerous enough to
attract attention, and offered a striking contrast to the other
red corpuscles about them, many of which were large, flattened
out, and less biconcave than usual.   A great variation in size
was noticed in all the specimens examined, and range as given
in the measurements, from $\frac{1}{3171}''$ to $\frac{1}{7000}''$ must be regarded as
very remarkable.   That these tiny elements are red corpuscles
there can be no doubt, as with No. 16 Hartnack (1-36th) they
appear homogeneous, of a pale yellow colour, and, like the larger
forms, are sometimes crenated.   In the third case reported in
Dr. Howard's paper on the subject,[*] the blood of which one of
us (Dr. O.) had an opportunity of examining in the spring of
1875, the note on the appearances of the blood is as follows :
" There is a somewhat unusual variation in size among the red
corpuscles, many of them scarcely measure the $\frac{1}{7000}$th part of
an inch in diameter.   The white corpuscles also present slight
variations in size and are more granular than normal.   Max
Schultze's granular masses are abundant."   Cohnheim, in a case
which will be more fully referred to hereafter, states that the
presence of the small blood corpuscles was established.   Quincke[†]
also speaks of the inequalities in the size of the red blood corpuscles, many of which were small and round.   In three of his
cases these smaller forms presented great irregularities in con-
tour.   These are, I believe, the only positive observations on
this point.   On the other hand, there is a note by Prof. Grainger
Stewart of Edinburgh,[‡] in which he states, that the blood in two
cases of pernicious anæmia, under treatment at the time, did
not present the small red corpuscles described by Eichorst.
Among recent cases in which the blood was carefully examined,

---

[*] Read before the International Medical Congress at Philadelphia, and
being published in the forthcoming Report.

[†] Volkmann's Sammlung Klinischer Vorträge, No. 100., translated in
Medical Times and Gazette, Oct. 14th, 1876.

[‡] Brit. Medical Journal, July 8th, 1876.

and no mention made either of small forms or great variations in size are those of Pepper,[*] Scheby-Buch,[†] Pye Smith,[‡] Lepine.[§] Bradford,[||] in his case, made a most careful examination of the blood, and reports not much variation in size, but that all are rather smaller than usual. In Ferrand's case[¶] many of the red blood corpuscles were larger than normal, no mention is made of any diminution in size. In Bradbury's case[**] the red corpuscles were larger than normal, pale, and exceedingly irregular in shape. No small forms were noticed. Burger[††] did not notice any great variations in size, but a peculiar paleness about them. Immermann[‡‡] makes no mention of alterations in form or size in the red corpuscles.

The presence of very small red disks in healthy blood is not common, still, one of us (Dr. O.) has occasionally measured forms not $\frac{1}{7000}$th of an inch in diameter, both in his own and in the blood of other quite healthy individuals. Laptschinsky[§§] has also found these small corpuscles in the blood of patients with various febrile affections, and speaks of them as being numerous, about $\frac{1}{3}$ the size of ordinary red corpuscles, some having an intensely red colour, whilst others are pale. In the blood from the above reported case, drawn in capillary tubes, and not examined until some hours after, many of the red corpuscles appear as deeply coloured spheres, slightly smaller than natural. This is a physical alteration, resulting apparently in a change from a disk-shape to a sphere, with, perhaps, a condensation of the corpuscle. These forms were not present in perfectly fresh blood, but could be seen in the slide six or eight hours

[*] Amer. Journal of Med. Sciences, Oct. 1875.

[†] Deutsches Archiv. f. Klin. Medicin, April, 1876.

[‡] Virchow's Archiv. Bd. 65. hft. 4. Dec. 1875.

[§] Bulletin General de Therapeutique, 30 Julliet, 1876.

[||] Boston Medical and Surgical Journal, May, 1876.

[¶] Bulletin General de Therapeutique, Dec. 15, 1876.

[**] Brit. Medical Journal, Dec. 30, 1876.

[††] Berliner Klin. Wochenschrift, No. 33, 1876.

[‡‡] Ziemssen's Handbuch der speciellen Path. and Therp. Bd. xiii. Art. Pro. Pernic. Anæm., 1875.

[§§] Centralblatt f. d. Med. Wissen. No. 42, 1874.

after mounting. It is interesting to remark with reference
to the large corpuscles, that Hayem[*] states that during a long
course of iron—just such as this man had been subjected to—
the red disks undergo an increase in volume.

Until we possess more definite knowledge than we do at present of the variation in size of the red corpuscles in constitutional
and febrile diseases, it would be hasty, from the limited number of
observations, to conclude that the presence of the small coloured
corpuscles is pathognomonic of, or even affords a positive diagnostic sign in, progressive pernicious anæmia. It remains for
subsequent observers to note accurately the size of the red
corpuscles in this disease, and it will not be long before we are
in a position to arrive at a satisfactory conclusion on this interesting point.

In a disease like pernicious anæmia, which after death is
is not characterized by any important lesion in the viscera
or glands, it was natural that attention should be directed to the
bone marrow, a structure now ranked among the blood-forming
organs, and which in leukæmia, and pseudo-leukæmia (anæmia
lymphatica, or Hodgkin's disease) has been found remarkably
altered, so much so that myelogenous forms of both have been
described. With the two affections just named the one in question is closely allied, and in its clinical features almost identical.
From the splenic and lymphatic forms of both, it is distinguished
by the absence of enlargement of the spleen and lymphatic
glands, and additionally from leukæmia by the failure of any
increase in the white blood corpuscles. In those rare cases of
leukæmia, where the disease is confined to the bone marrow—
myelogenous form—the only distinguishing feature is the excess-
ive number of colourless corpuscles in the blood, with, perhaps,
tenderness over the affected bones (Mosler). Immermann[†]
quotes a case in illustration of this. In the still rarer cases of
myelogenous pseudo-leukæmia, where the affection is uncomplicated with disease of the spleen or lymphatic glands, a differential
diagnosis would be impossible, (compare the remarkable cases

* Bulletin General de Therapeutique, Dec. 15th 1876.
† Loc. Cit. p. 651.

given by Wood*). It is not to be wondered at that some writers (Immermann and Jaccoud†) should hint at the identity of the two diseases, or that Pepper, encouraged by the appearance of the marrow in one of his cases, should state that progressive pernicious anæmia was " merely the simple medullary form of pseudo-leukæmia."

The evidence of an implication of the marrow in this disease rests upon the following reports : the first case in which it was examined was one of Pepper's, in which the marrow of the radius and sternum was " made up almost entirely of small granular cells." Passing over a case observed by Fede,‡ and recorded as one of pernicious anæmia, but which ought to be regarded as a well-marked myelogenous pseudo-leukæmia, the next observation is by Scheby-Buch,§ in one of whose cases the marrow of the radius was pale red in colour, and contained numerous cells like white blood corpuscles, and very few red corpuscles or fat cells. In Lepine's‖ case nothing unusual was found. Burger¶ states that there was no affection of the marrow in his case. By far the most extended account of the changes in the marrow in this disease is that given by Cohnheim in a letter to Virchow.** The following is a summary of the appearances described : Marrow of all the bones intensely red ; fat almost entirely absent. Microscopically there were (1), ordinary marrow cells of various sizes, some small and lymphoid in character, others large and with vesicular nuclei : (2.) coloured elements in almost equal number, of these the common, biconcave, red blood corpuscles formed a decided minority, while the number of red non-nucleated corpuscles of various dimensions was very evident. The smallest of these had the diameter of normal red blood corpuscles, the largest were more than

* Am. Journ. of Medical Sciences, Oct. 1871.
† Nouv. Dict. de Med. et de Chirurg. Leucocythémie.
‡ Quoted in Centralblatt, f. die Med. Wissen., Oct. 16th, 1875.
§ Loc. cit.
‖ Loc. cit.
¶ Loc. cit. No. 34, 1876.
** Virchow, Archiv. Bd. lxviii, Hft., 2. Oct, 26, 1876.

double the size of colourless blood corpuscles, and between them forms intermediate in size. (3.) Nucleated red corpuscles in great abundance, and of various sizes, the majority equalling in size the smaller of the true marrow cells. The blood examined after death was also found to contain a few of the nucleated red corpuscles. In Quincke's article no details are given, and this part of the question is disposed of with the remark: "The marrow of the bone showed no abnormality." In Bradbury's case, the red marrow from the right tibia looked natural, and was made up almost entirely of granular spheroidal cells, like white blood corpuscles. In that from the sternum the cells were much larger, and red globules more abundant. Coloured corpuscles were not numerous.

These are the only facts for and against the view that pernicious anæmia is the medullary form of pseudo-leukæmia. The general statement of Quincke, and the more definite ones of Lepine and Burger, are not very satisfactory, as no details are given ; still, they must be accepted as negative evidence. It may be held with Bradbury* that the changes in the marrow of the sternum and radius in Pepper's case were scarcely sufficient to indicate serious disease of that structure, as only the normal elements were found, though in the radius in slightly increased numbers, and the same may be said of Scheby-Buch's case. In Cohnheim's case and our own the constitution of the medulla was altered, and, in addition to ordinary marrow cells, it contained lymphoid corpuscles, embryonal forms,† and red blood corpuscles of various sizes. The detection, too, in both, of the embryonal forms in the blood, though in quite insignificant numbers, places them apart from the others ; and on these grounds they alone are strictly comparable with myelogenous leukæmia. Indeed, the question at once arises whether we have not to do here with

---

* Loc Cit.

† In a recent note in the Archiv. f. Mikroscop. Anatomie, Bd. xii. p. 796, Neumann expresses a wish that the term "transitional," as applied to the nucleated red corpuscles, should be dropped, as involving an hypothesis about their origin, advanced rather too confidently by him. He would substitute the term "embryonal" or "developmental" form.

an uncomplicated case of medullary pseudo-leukæmia, similar to one of those described by Wood[*]. A consideration of the symptoms will not help us, and the remarkable admission must be made, that while the ante-mortem diagnosis of pernicious anæmia was correct, a post-mortem one of pseudo-leukæmia might be equally so.

The absence of these changes in the marrow in the cases of Quincke, Lepine, and Burger proves that the disease in certain cases is independent of any affection of this structure ; and we must either regard implication of the marrow as an accidental complication, having but little to do with the cause or progress of the disease, or refer all cases in which it is met with to the category of myelogenous affections. Can the state of the marrow be regarded as an accidental complication, a secondary change, depending on the grave constitutional disease ? Our knowledge of the condition of this tissue in disease is not at all complete, and the only observations at hand on the subject are the following :

Neumann[†] met with great hyperplasia of the marrow in a case of Addison's disease.

Wood, in a paper already referred to, says, that he has " made a number of examinations of long bones taken from patients dead of various chronic diseases, and never, except in a single case, found any abundance of the leucocytes ;" and this was probably a case of leukæmia.

In 14 examinations made by Dr. Osler of the marrow of the long bones, obtained chiefly from chronic Hospital cases, in only one was there found hyperplasia and marked alteration in its constitution ; and in this instance there is a strong probability of the case belonging to the group under consideration.

Altogether, the few facts we have are opposed to the view that in chronic diseases, accompanied with anæmia and wasting, hyperplasia of the marrow of the long bones occurs as a secondary change.

Cohnheim[‡] writing to Virchow, on his case, says, " You will

---

[*] Loc. Cit. p. 293.
[†] Quoted in Quarterly Journal of Microscopy, 1871.
[‡] Loc. Cit. p 382.

Ingram Content Group UK Ltd.
Milton Keynes UK
UKHW022330050623
422929UK00005B/206

9 781016 232715